God Wraps Our

Family

In Love

God Wraps Our

Family

In Love

Volume 2

Farley Dunn

THIS IS A MYCHURCHNOTES.NET BOOK

PUBLISHED BY MYCHURCHNOTES.NET
AND THREE SKILLET PUBLISHING
(www.ThreeSkilletPublishing.com)

COPYRIGHT © 2018 BY FARLEY DUNN

www.mychurchnotes.net

God Wraps Our Family in Love /Farley Dunn – 1st ed.

Vol. 2

This is an original work created by
Farley Dunn for the website MyChurchNotes.net.

All rights reserved.
ISBN: 978-1-943189-61-8

Non-public domain scripture quotations are from The Holy Bible, English Standard Version® (ESV®), copyright © 2001 by Crossway, a publishing ministry of Good News Publishers. Used by permission. All rights reserved.

Dedication

To my wife and son for the hours I've been allowed to spend at my computer.

MyChurchNotes.net

Table of Contents

Buttressed Against the World	19
Caring for Our Own	23
Childhood Lessons	27
Choosing the Savior	31
Forming a Good Fit	37
Friend or Foe?	43
Getting Straight with God	49
Holding Our Anger	55
Honor in the House	59
If I Die Before I Wake	65
Keeping Out of Trouble	71
Love by Example	75
Onto the Mountaintop	79
Our Reason for Relationship	85
Our Responsibility in Christ	91
Our Small Requirement	95
Our Vote of Approval	99
Reassessing Our Gifts	103
Sitting in the Child's Seat	107
Submitted to God	113
Surviving God's Fire	119
Taking Care of the Little Guy	125
The Highest Honor	131
Train Up a Child	137
Two Peas Make a Pod	143
Weaving Love Into Our Lives	149
When We Fall in Love	155
Coming to Christ in Three Easy Steps	159

Introduction

God has established our family as our basis for our self-worth and ongoing self-care system.

Our family is our fortress against the world. When we are battered by what life brings against us, our redoubt is unearthed in the people who are most closely bonded with us.

Our family.

It's important to learn to live in harmony with those we love, to tweak our relationships until we can co-exist in the peace found only through Jesus, our spiritual advisor, example and king. We must first submit to God, then we can take care of each other. We can weave love into our lives and fall in love with each other all over again.

It's our reason for relationship, to love and support

one another.

Let's get straight with God, hold in our anger when times get rough, and know that through the care we've shown them, we've paid the highest honor to the ones we love.

We'll receive God's vote of approval when we do.

Farley Dunn

Light Bulb Moment

When we stand together, we stand tall in Christ.

Buttressed Against the World

To be on a pedestal is a difficult place to be.

You see, it's the way the pedestal is constructed. It's a single piece, with no buttresses to support it. All it takes is a good bump, and down it goes, us with it, to crash to the ground, skinned elbows and all.

Our support buttresses come from the people we love and who love us in return. When we are intertwined with other people, we build a support structure that can stand the test of time.

Ephesians 4:2-3 tells us that relational strength comes from our gentle way of dealing with each other's shortcomings:

> "With all humility and gentleness, with patience, bearing with one another in love, eager to maintain the unity of the Spirit in the bond of peace."

Colossians 3:14 places love as the sturdiest buttress we can build. With it, we are stronger than we can ever be alone:

> "And above all these put on love, which binds everything together in perfect harmony."

Ecclesiastes 4:9-11 reveals the asset that comes with two. We find our strength in those at our side:

> "Two are better than one, because they have a good reward for their toil. For if they fall, one will lift up his fellow. But woe to him who is alone when he falls and has not another to lift him up! Again, if two lie together, they keep warm, but how can one keep warm alone?"

Ephesians 5:25 holds up our marriage in the light of Christ's death on the cross. He died for us. We can afford to do no less for our beloved spouse, if we truly hold him or her in the highest level of love:

> "Husbands, love your wives, as Christ loved the church and gave himself up for her."

To stand alone in good times is easy. It's the wind that tests our spirits, and the waves that batter our souls. Our buttress of protection is found in those who stand at our side, enduring it all with us.

When we stand together, we stand tall in Christ.

Light Bulb Moment

The love of Christ becomes most apparent when we share it daily.

Caring for Our Own

We look across the world at devastations that move us to help.

An earthquake in Mexico. Volcanic activity in Indonesia. Drought in Africa.

All these are worthy projects for us to jump into, for our aid will improve others' lives. That's commendable and an admirable goal for each of us to take on.

We must be careful not to ignore those who live at our side, while we are helping those far away.

Leviticus 19:18 sets our standard for dealing with those around us:

> "You shall not take vengeance or bear a grudge against the sons of your own people, but you shall love your neighbor as yourself: I am the Lord."

Who are our people? Our families, for certain. Our

spouse and our children, uncles and aunts. Our church families, also, those we worship with, sing alongside in the choir, and greet on Sunday morning.

Our neighbors and community leaders, also. We can't forget about them. We must be as concerned about the people within our proximity as we are for those far away.

We must love our neighbors as ourselves. Our example is Christ, for he took of his time and energy to offer himself to the people walking at his side.

The love of Christ becomes most apparent when we share it daily.

Light Bulb Moment

When we live like Christ, we can be sure our example is one we're proud for our children to follow.

Childhood Lessons

We want our children to be a reflection of us.

Well, parts of us, the good parts we don't mind sharing with the world.

It's that "do as I say and not as I do" thing that's so easy to fall back on. It's easier to tell our children how to live than it is to show them the way we should live.

Proverbs 21:21 shows us the path we should set our feet on, if we want to raise children we can be proud of.

> "Whoever pursues righteousness and kindness will find life, righteousness, and honor."

There's the example we should set for our children. It's a two-step process, and if we follow it, our kiddos will turn out right as rain.

First, we must live in a right manner. Pay our

taxes. Follow the traffic laws. Not cheat our employees . . . You're getting it!

Second, be kind in all things. Be nice to the server at the restaurant. Even when the service is poor. Even when we don't like the food. Be kind. In all things. To everyone . . . This one's harder, isn't it?

If we do these two things, we'll be rewarded with life, righteousness, and honor, and we'll be proud when our children turn out just like us.

When we live like Christ, we can be sure our example is one we're proud for our children to follow.

Light Bulb Moment

We may not get to choose our family, but Jesus gets to choose his, and he's already chosen us.

Choosing the Savior

We get to choose our friends, but our family? Ha! We're stuck with them. Family comes already imbued with fractures, contentious history, and the ability to suck the life out of every holiday.

Carine Fabius at huffingtonpost.com talks about "the anxiety of having to be around the family you do have when all may not be love and light with certain members of the crew."

The Bible says we are sons of God, the children of Jehovah, and co-heirs with Christ. Siblings. Brothers and sisters in the Lord to the extent that some churches today still refer to their membership with those time-worn honorifics.

Yet, we are the chosen of God. He reached out and picked us one at a time. Fractures in the kingdom? God desires us to be solid as a rock. Contentious history? Christianity is about loving those we're with. Sucking the life out of other people's days?

We're to infuse life into everyone we meet.

So, which end of the whirly-gig are we attached to, the family end, filled with fractures, contention, and lifeless holidays, or the friend end, full of love and light?

John 15:16 is our assurance that Jesus wanted each one of us to be part of his kingdom.

> "You did not choose me, but I chose you and appointed you that you should go and bear fruit and that your fruit should abide, so that whatever you ask the Father in my name, he may give it to you."

Ephesians 1:4-5 tells us that not only are we chosen as friends of our Lord, he goes one step further and begins the adoption process to make us part of his family.

> "Even as he chose us in him before the foundation of the world, that we should be holy and blameless before him. In love he predestined us for adoption as sons through Jesus Christ, according to the purpose of his will."

Romans 8:28-30 reveals the glorious nature of our new family.

> "And we know that for those who love God all things work together for good, for those who are

called according to his purpose. For those whom he foreknew he also predestined to be conformed to the image of his Son, in order that he might be the firstborn among many brothers. And those whom he predestined he also called, and those whom he called he also justified, and those whom he justified he also glorified."

This is indeed the best of every scenario. The most enjoyable people in the world are chosen to be part of our family so that we can enjoy our time with them. Imagine choosing our favorite people from anyone we wish, and imagine assembling them into our ideal family. Jesus has already done that. He predestined us for adoption as sons through Jesus Christ. He assembled us as the ideal family before time began, and now all we have to do is make the choice to follow after him.

It's time for us to choose our Savior so that we can take our rightful place in our Christian family. Once we do, all will be love and light, no matter who's part of our crew.

We may not get to choose our family, but Jesus gets to choose his, and he's already chosen us.

Light Bulb Moment

When we come together, God will shape us perfectly to be stronger than we were alone.

Forming a Good Fit

The best things in life are well-constructed.

Take a top-notch car. Panel gaps will be even, the stitching on the seats will lie flat, and the engine will start smoothly every time.

If any of these things fail to perform, the car will sell abysmally, and the line will be quickly discontinued.

The DeLorean was an incredible gull-winged sports car with an all-aluminum body. It was slow and overpriced, and the company folded due to cost and logistics pressures.

GM's Geo line was formed to battle small imports from Suzuki, Isuzu, and Toyota. However, even being cheap and economical didn't help it survive as an independent car line when people demanded better built and more luxurious rides.

Even with the best intentions, our plan must form a good fit with the needs of others, or our efforts will ultimately fail.

Genesis 2:24 tells us we can find our perfect fit in each other if we abandon all other distractions:

> "Therefore a man shall leave his father and his mother and hold fast to his wife, and they shall become one flesh."

Ecclesiastes 4:12 says our strength comes from being wrapped in the bonds of love:

> "And though a man might prevail against one who is alone, two will withstand him—a threefold cord is not quickly broken."

Mark 10:9 cautions against tearing apart our most intimate connections:

> "What therefore God has joined together, let not man separate."

Ephesians 5:25-33 lays out the steps for building a strong marriage, one that will fit a man perfectly to a woman, and stand the test of time:

> "Husbands, love your wives, as Christ loved the church and gave himself up for her, that he might sanctify her, having cleansed her by the washing of water with the word, so that he might present the church to himself in splendor, without spot or wrinkle or any such thing, that

she might be holy and without blemish. In the same way husbands should love their wives as their own bodies. He who loves his wife loves himself. For no one ever hated his own flesh, but nourishes and cherishes it, just as Christ does the church, because we are members of his body. 'Therefore a man shall leave his father and mother and hold fast to his wife, and the two shall become one flesh.' This mystery is profound, and I am saying that it refers to Christ and the church. However, let each one of you love his wife as himself, and let the wife see that she respects her husband."

When we put time and effort into our relationships, we'll find we craft a better marriage, and we will be able to survive the stresses of life no matter what tries to destroy our love.

When we come together, God will shape us perfectly to be stronger than we were alone.

Light Bulb Moment

We can love our friends, but our true strength comes from our family.

Friend or Foe?

We might better title this essay Friend or Family. But then, that would be rather tacky.

Yet, the Word tells us that's exactly how we need to view our friends and family.

Proverbs 17:17 tells us:

> "A friend loves at all times, and a brother is born for adversity."

Let's look at the last half of this verse. What exactly does the phrase "a brother is born for adversity" mean? Are we to understand that a brother will always rub us the wrong way?

Different commentaries have vastly different opinions.

The Benson Commentary says that our relations are here to comfort us in our adversity.

Matthew Henry's Concise Commentary tells us that

only Christ can be a true friend.

Barnes' Notes on the Bible says that a friend becomes a brother in adversity.

Matthew Poole's Commentary suggests we are reborn into the role of a brother when adversity comes our way.

Cambridge Bible for Schools and Colleges says it like this: A friend made in the time of adversity becomes closer than a brother.

There is another way to read Psalms 17:17. It's in the admonition spoken by Jesus.

Matthew 13:57 reveals his thoughts to us.

> "But Jesus said to them, 'A prophet is not without honor except in his hometown and in his own household.' "

It's yin and yang. Friend versus foe. Me against you. Contention between the people closest to us. Often we find support in our friends, even as we fight at family get-togethers.

We want to cast our family aside. Truly. Dump them on the side of the road, because our friends love us better.

1 Timothy 5:8 tells us differently.

"But if anyone does not provide for his relatives, and especially for members of his household, he has denied the faith and is worse than an unbeliever."

The reality of our lives may indeed be that we need our friends to support us, because we find only foes in our family. However, we cannot cast our family on the trash heap. They are ours, regardless of the adversity they show to us.

Perhaps Friend or Family is the best title for this essay after all. Our friends are great for our ego, and we need them around. Our family is who we are, and we need them even more. They are the ones who will stand beside us when all others fall away, even when we rub each other the wrong way.

We can love our friends, but our true strength comes from our family.

Light Bulb Moment

When we come to Christ, he changes all of us, even the parts no one else sees.

Getting Straight with God

The plan of salvation is a simple one. We believe in Christ, our sins are forgiven, and we follow after him. In fact, the plan is so simple we sometimes forget God has expectations of us.

Yes, God has things he requires us to do. Well, duh, we groan. That's obvious. And it is, but just what's obvious?

We can't sin anymore. We understand that one. No more drunken binges. We can't cheat on our taxes. We must treat our neighbors kindly and with respect. Love. There must be lots of love shown through good manners, helping others, and general generosity toward the less fortunate.

Is that all? How about our personal habits? Or is that private? Our waistline is personal. Our bank accounts are no one else's business. The state of our closets? No one can tell us to organize the interior of our home. Back off, buster! We may be

Christian, but that's crossing a line!

We need to take a look at Ezra 8:33-34 to see how God views the "personal" parts of our lives.

> "Now on the fourth day was the silver and the gold and the vessels weighed in the House of our God by the hand of Meremoth the son of Uriah the Priest; and with him was Eleazar the son of Phinehas; and with them was Jozabad the son of Jeshua, and Noadiah the son of Binnui, Levites; by number and by weight of every one: and all the weight was written at that time."

To truly picture the impact of this passage, we need to understand the context. The children of Israel had just arrived in Jerusalem after seventy years of captivity. They were exhausted. Three days of rest? Bah! They'd walked the entire trip. They needed three years to recuperate.

Yet the Word says that on the fourth day, they weighed the gold and the silver, and they recorded all the weight.

To say it in modern terms, they got home from work, and they hung up their coat, put the groceries away, and took time to fix a proper meal. They did what was necessary rather than putting it off to another day.

So, when will we start that diet? Organize that closet? Mow the back yard? That's not me, we cry. That's right. It's not us. It's God. He's the one we need to get straight with. He wants all of who we are to exemplify his nature, including that which is hidden from public view.

When we come to Christ, he changes all of us, even the parts no one else sees.

Light Bulb Moment

Following Christ is sometimes in what we don't do. Let's show his love through our kindness toward others.

Holding Our Anger

Speaking our minds is often a sure-fire way to get into trouble.

We've all done it, spoken before we considered how it would sound. We've dealt with the backlash, too, when we've angered those around us.

When it happens with a boss or a spouse, it's especially devastating. They can mete out consequences that make us want to retract everything we said.

James 1:19 gives us an easy solution.

> "Know this, my beloved brothers: let every person be quick to hear, slow to speak, slow to anger."

The three things James tells us are interlinked. Let's break them down.

"Quick to hear."

This is the simple one. We must practice good

listening skills. Let someone finish what they're saying. Acknowledge what they've said so they know they've been heard.

"Slow to speak."

This is more difficult. Sometimes we need to bite our tongues. We don't need to say everything that comes to us. If it's really important, it will wait until tomorrow. It will. Trust me.

"Slow to anger."

Now we're to the tough one. There are things we need to set aside. See how we feel tomorrow. Does it still make us angry? Many times, when the moment passes, so does the emotion. It's important not to stir up things that will become unimportant if we let them go.

Following Christ is sometimes in what we don't do. Let's show his love through our kindness toward others.

Light Bulb Moment

When we are rooted in Christ, we will bloom before the world with the sincerity of his love.

Honor in the House

Our family gives us roots. In the epic 1977 miniseries *Roots*, we learned about African teen Kunta Kinte, who found himself enslaved in America. His roots ran deep, stretching across the ocean to a distant continent. And yet, he put down roots in his new life, also, ones honored in the film.

Yet, there is such a thing as false honor, something we heap on ourselves to make ourselves seem better than we are, better than our history, better than our roots make us out to be.

We shame ourselves in the process.

Matthew 23:5 tells us:

> "They do all their deeds to be seen by others. For they make their phylacteries broad and their fringes long."

The passage goes on to say that they love their place of honor at banquets and want to be seen in the chief seats in the synagogues.

Who are they? Specifically, the Scribes and Pharisees. More aptly? The modern day Christian.

De we want the solo in the choir because we wish to share in ministry, or because we feel we're better than the other singers around us? If our name's not listed on the overhead screen during church member appreciation night, are our feelings hurt? Or do we rejoice in those who receive praise?

If our roots are firmly planted in Jesus, in our salvation, and in the cross, we won't need to raise ourselves up with the false honor of banquets and chief seats. We won't desire to have our name splashed across the church's video screens.

Instead let's think of the movie that will be made of our life in 50 years' time. Will it portray family, honor, and a person who works hard for Christ, while demanding nothing other than that all praise be diverted unto the Father above, the one who deserves all honor and glory and praise?

Matthew 6:6 tells us how it's done:

> "But when you pray, go into your room and shut the door and pray to your Father who is in secret. And your Father who sees in secret will reward you."

Honor from the Father is true honor, and it builds us up before the world. We don't have to seek it. It comes to us when we follow after him.

When we are rooted in Christ, we will bloom before the world with the sincerity of his love.

Light Bulb Moment

When we come to the cross, Jesus lifts us into new life, awaking us from the sleep of sin and decay.

If I Die Before I Wake

The words from Psalm 4:8 are the basis for *A Child's First Prayer,* published in 1884, in a song attributed to an unknown author, with a melody by Hubert P. Main. The words are simple, but the meaning is not.

Now I lay me down to sleep,

I pray the Lord my soul to keep;

If I should die before I wake,

I pray the Lord my soul to take;

And this I ask for Jesus' sake.

Sleep in this prayer has multiple meanings. We can look at it as: 1. resting the eyes during a restorative period each day; 2. a time of spiritual unawareness; 3. the span between physical death and spiritual reawakening in Christ.

It's all in the context in which we find the word.

Now I lay me down to sleep . . .

From a child's viewpoint, we see a tyke's room, with horses and clouds on the walls, and a nightlight glowing in the corner. It's a peaceful scene, that of a small girl or boy snoozing the midnight hour away.

From God's viewpoint, we are drowsing through the most important hours of our days. We are spiritually asleep. His alarm clock went off 2,000 years ago on a cross on Golgotha. He's been attempting to rouse us ever since.

1 Thessalonians 4:13-16 starts off:

> "But we do not want you to be uninformed, brothers, about those who are asleep, that you may not grieve as others do who have no hope."

Paul speaks of those who have died, but his words fit equally well on the shoulders of those who have yet to recognize the authority of Christ over our world. Our hope comes in Verse 16:

> "For the Lord himself will descend from heaven with a cry of command, with the voice of an archangel, and with the sound of the trumpet of God. And the dead in Christ will rise first."

Let's return to our 1884 song. *If I should die before I*

wake . . .

This hits close to home. If our unsaved friends and family refuse to accept Christ as their savior, this becomes their sinkhole of despair. What will happen to them once they are gone?

We find our answer for those who have accepted the salvation of Christ in the words of Psalm 4:8:

> "In peace I will both lie down and sleep; for you alone, O Lord, make me dwell in safety."

Let's read the last line of that old hymn once more. *And this I ask for Jesus' sake*. Our job is to keep our loved ones held continually before the throne. We are to be the example that emulates the love of Christ so that Jesus can entreat them to come to him.

When we live the example of Christ, our faith in our God's redeeming power will make an amazing difference in the lives of those we care most about.

When we come to the cross, Jesus lifts us into new life, awaking us from the sleep of sin and decay.

Light Bulb Moment

With our eyes focused on God, we won't be bothered by the trouble just outside our door.

Keeping Out of Trouble

No one steps in mud on purpose.

Or falls off the dock or burns their hand.

They're called accidents for a reason. They are unintentional, and we avoid them whenever possible.

Yet, some adrenalin junkies push as close to the edge as possible, just for the thrill of it. We can go online and watch videos of 4-wheelers gunning their way over deadly terrain. They often make it unscathed, but some go bottoms up.

Skiers risk avalanches every day. It doesn't make them stay away.

Formula One drivers run at breakneck speed with dozens of other cars a handbreadth apart. They seem to be asking for trouble.

Proverbs 26:17 describes our risky behavior.

"Whoever meddles in a quarrel not his own is

like one who takes a passing dog by the ears."

Are we the adrenalin junkie that jumps in and gets involved in others' disputes? Have we grabbed the dog's ears, only to have it turn and snap at us? Have we lost sight of our family values and taken on problems that aren't ours to shoulder?

4-wheel vehicles are built to protect their drivers. Skiers carry avalanche kits, where they can be found if the worst happens. Even Formula One drivers are safer than you might imagine, as modern safety measures allow them to walk away from the most horrific crashes.

We never walk away unscathed from disputes we should have never meddled in. Our family can be our buffer zone. We can keep out of trouble when we keep our nose clean by focusing on our family and minding God's business, not that of people around us.

With our eyes focused on God, we won't be bothered by the trouble just outside our door.

Love is learned by example, and our finest example is Christ.

Love by Example

Every generation learns anew.

Everything: manners; self-control; monetary principles.

We build on the knowledge of our forebears, but we must learn how to operate within the confines of our society just like our parents did.

We can help our children shortcut many of the problems of being the upcoming generation.

Ephesians 6:4 reveals the way:

> "Fathers, do not provoke your children to anger, but bring them up in the discipline and instruction of the Lord."

Do not provoke . . . means to be kind, to be patient, and to understand what it means to be young. Kids don't have it all figured out, and they will make mistakes. Help them through without yelling.

Bring them up in the discipline and instruction of the Lord . . . means we need to live our lives by the Lord's principles. That's how our children learn about God, by seeing him through our behaviors.

Our children learn what we teach them. Everything. Let's teach them of God, so that they will know the Lord in the fullness of who he is.

Love is learned by example, and our finest example is Christ.

Light Bulb Moment

When we come off the mountain, the love of God carries us home.

Onto the Mountaintop

A trio of mountain bikers took off in 2012 to find the highest mountains in the world to ride their bikes.

Were they crazy, or what?

They started in Utah, which has some of the best dirt trails in North America. It was their home base, and had been for years. They packed their bikes to the top for the thrill of the speed as they came down. Yet, one day they showed up to ride, and it felt ordinary. Fifty, sixty miles-per-hour, with jumps that left nothing between them and the ground but air . . . and it felt ordinary.

These men wanted something bigger, something grander, a place that had never seen a mountain bike before. These three amigos wanted it all.

They traveled to China and South America, climbing until the air was so thin they could barely breathe, and then to the Rocky Mountains of British Columbia, where helicopters took them even higher. Every trip was filled with new thrills. Yet, at the end of their journeys, they found themselves back where they started, in the high mountains of Utah.

Isaiah 43:19 tells us:

> "Behold, I am doing a new thing; now it springs forth, do you not perceive it? I will make a way in the wilderness and rivers in the desert."

We don't need to travel the world to find something new. God is bringing it to us. It's up to us to be prepared and ever watchful, so that God's new thing doesn't pass us by.

Psalm 127:3 tells us:

> "Behold, children are a heritage from the Lord, the fruit of the womb a reward."

What a delight we can find in our children! Rather than view them as a hindrance to our joy, let's see them as the source of our happiness. God views us the same way. Even when we encumber him, he finds his delight in us.

John 1:1-5 tells us:

> "In the beginning was the Word, and the Word was with God, and the Word was God. He was in

the beginning with God. All things were made through him, and without him was not anything made that was made. In him was life, and the life was the light of men. The light shines in the darkness, and the darkness has not overcome it."

We can head to the mountaintops, and we will find excitement there. However, those three mountain bikers found a new joy in their Utah mountains after traveling the world. They saw it with fresh eyes, and it became theirs again.

There are times we want to be on the mountaintop, yet we don't consider what we're leaving behind. When we've finished with our mountaintop experience, let's not forget that the place we left is just behind us, and that's where our joy needs to be found.

When we come off the mountain, the love of God carries us home.

Light Bulb Moment

When we devote ourselves to our spouse, we become closer to Christ in the process.

Our Reason for Relationship

What's so important about each other?

Why do we need to be married in the first place?

It sometimes seems we'd be better off doing our own thing in our own way. No arguments, no divorce, and never any giving up what we want for the silly things someone else thinks important.

Yet, God feels differently. When creating humanity, he had a plan. Part of that plan was for relationships to meet inbred needs in each of us.

Genesis 1:27-28 reveals the core of our relationship function. Together we are powerful enough to conquer the whole world.

> "So God created man in his own image, in the image of God he created him; male and female he created them. And God blessed them. And God said to them, 'Be fruitful and multiply and fill the earth and subdue it and have dominion

over the fish of the sea and over the birds of the heavens and over every living thing that moves on the earth.' "

Malachi 2:14-15 lays out the legacy of a good marriage. We instill the faith of our God in our children when we keep our relationship vows from our youth.

> "But you say, 'Why does he not?' Because the LORD was witness between you and the wife of your youth, to whom you have been faithless, though she is your companion and your wife by covenant. Did he not make them one, with a portion of the Spirit in their union? And what was the one God seeking? Godly offspring. So guard yourselves in your spirit, and let none of you be faithless to the wife of your youth."

Isaiah 54:5 compares our earthly relationships with the spiritual bond we have with God. We are to look upon our spouse as the one who provides us unconditional emotional support and an abiding love.

> "For your Maker is your husband, the LORD of hosts is his name; and the Holy One of Israel is your Redeemer, the God of the whole earth he is called."

Song of Solomon 8:6-7 reveals true love as a consuming flame that cannot be quenched by desire for status, material wealth, or personal gain. When we truly love, it erases our desire for everything else.

> "Set me as a seal upon your heart, as a seal upon your arm, for love is strong as death, jealousy is fierce as the grave. Its flashes are flashes of fire, the very flame of the LORD. Many waters cannot quench love, neither can floods drown it. If a man offered for love all the wealth of his house, he would be utterly despised."

God has a reason for marriage. It's not a situational thing, good for some people and not for others. We need sincere, unbreakable connections with other people, relationships that delve into the core of our being, ones we can trust with the truth of who we really are.

When we devote ourselves to our spouse, we become closer to Christ in the process.

Light Bulb Moment

When we accept our Christian responsibility, we become the nurturer our family needs to see in us.

Our Responsibility in Christ

Duty.

That's a word no one wants to hear.

Merriam-Webster tells us it's a form of respect; an obligatory task; a moral or legal obligation.

Webster's also says it's something we're assigned to do; our responsibility.

So, what is our responsibility? What are we, as Christians, required to do?

1 Timothy 5:8 doesn't leave us much wriggle room.

> "But if anyone does not provide for his relatives, and especially for members of his household, he has denied the faith and is worse than an unbeliever."

We are to be filled with love, preach the gospel, and give generously to the poor. We're to treat our neighbors as ourselves. These are part of our Christian walk. However, if we do all these things and don't provide for our father, our mother, our siblings, our spouse, and our children, we've denied the power of Christ and our redemption though him.

Let's return to Webster's for a moment. Duty is a form of respect, in addition to something we're assigned to do. When we respect our family, we will provide for them as proof of our faith in Christ.

When we accept our Christian responsibility, we become the nurturer our family needs to see in us.

Light Bulb Moment

When we step up for God, he will step up for us.

Our Small Requirement

Responsibility can be overwhelming.

We have our family to care for, bills to pay, and we can't let our retirement planning slip for even one day.

Then there's our house to maintain, the family car, and investments to watch over.

We haven't even gotten to our church and the time we must volunteer there. How can we get it all done?

God's requirement is simple. We find it in Micah 6:8.

> "He has told you, O man, what is good; and what does the Lord require of you but to do justice, and to love kindness, and to walk humbly with your God?"

We are asked to do three things to stand fulfilled

before God.

> 1. We must be fair and show justice to those around us. That includes paying our bills, honoring our promises, and maintaining a strong ethical standard.
>
> 2. We must be kind in our words and actions. That means speaking gently, being considerate, and being aware of what makes life better for others.
>
> 3. We are to be humble before God. Pride in accomplishments has no place in the Christian's life. All honor must be given to God for everything we achieve.

God doesn't expect us to be superhuman. He only wants us to be fair, kind, and humble, especially to our family. That's not too much to expect from the God of all creation.

When we step up for God, he will step up for us.

Light Bulb Moment

When we know we're loved, our feeling of approval is always there.

Our Vote of Approval

Good parenting doesn't mean we constantly applaud our children.

If we go overboard in the praise arena, our kids become callous to our enthusiasm, and it takes an ever-higher level of praise to evoke an emotional response.

Most of life is doing ordinary things, mundane activities that are our baseline for the bright moments of excitement and praise that punctuate our existence and make it worthwhile.

We soak in the praise, and then we get back to what we were doing.

1 Samuel 26:25 reveals this in practice in the life of David.

> "Then Saul said to David, 'Blessed be you, my son David! You will do many things and will succeed in them.' So David went his way, and Saul

returned to his place."

Saul didn't require daily parades and celebratory events on a weekly basis in order to get his message across. He gave David his vote of approval in a few simple words, and they both returned to the business of the day.

The key concept we should take away from this is that we must celebrate the successes of our spouse, our children, and our coworkers. Our words of praise need to be special, however, and that means we can't overdo it.

Our love must be constant. Our praise is for the special times when we need to lift someone's spirit so they will know they have our vote of approval.

When we know we're loved, our feeling of approval is always there.

Light Bulb Moment

When our focus is on Jesus, our love for the world will melt away.

Reassessing Our Gifts

Ownership can mute our enjoyment of things.

We become caught up in paying the bills for repairs or having to juggle our time spent in maintenance.

We look at our new car and despair at the payment each month.

The drive to our new, high-paying job becomes burdensome.

We grow tired of cleaning our McMansion.

The yearly vacation becomes a chore rather than a pleasure.

It's important for us to step back to get a better view of what we own. Psalm 90:12 is our vantage point.

> "So teach us to number our days that we may get a heart of wisdom."

To number our days means to think about things and their value to us. How will these items increase our quality of life? If they don't, it's wisdom to toss them out.

Sell the car.

Work a more practical job.

Move to a manageable house.

Plan a vacation closer to home, one that everyone can enjoy.

We can pick and choose the gifts we've been given to decide what will enhance our lives. We don't need to cling to all of them. Sometimes the best thing for our Christian walk is to focus on God and let him be the enjoyment in our days.

When our focus is on Jesus, our love for the world will melt away.

Light Bulb Moment

When we follow the training we get from God, we will mature in the image of God.

Sitting in the Child's Seat

Being a parent is all about responsibility. We have a duty to house, clothe, and feed the little ones we bring into the world. We are the people who must set the example we want our children to follow.

Ethan Couch was a wealthy Texas teenager in 2013 when his truck hit another car, killing four people and leaving one of his best friends a near-vegetable. His defense attorney claimed "affluenza," that Ethan's wealth prevented him from understanding the consequences of his actions. He received ten years' probation.

In 2015 Ethan broke his probation; and he and his mother disappeared, effectively dismantling his defense.

Proverbs 22:6 tells us:

> "Train up a child in the way he should go; even when he is old he will not depart from it."

What if we train a child in the wrong way? Will he continue to travel that road also? Part of Ethan's defense was that he was unmonitored as a young teen, without curfews or limits set on his activities.

Proverbs 29:15 says:

> "The rod and reproof give wisdom, but a child left to himself brings shame to his mother."

The "rod and reproof" stand for the curfews and limits we set on our children. They are our guide, our set of instructions for how we want them to behave as adults.

Perhaps we need to pay attention to these three verses:

Romans 8:16 reminds us of our place in the scheme of things:

> "The Spirit himself bears witness with our spirit that we are children of God."

Ephesians 6:4 is our instruction to raise our charges in a responsible manner:

> "Fathers, do not provoke your children to anger, but bring them up in the discipline and instruction of the Lord."

Mark 9:42 illustrates the gravity of getting it wrong:

"Whoever causes one of these little ones who believe in me to sin, it would be better for him if a great millstone were hung around his neck and he were thrown into the sea."

Let's sit in our child's seat. Let's take a moment to see the world from his viewpoint. Let's see our leadership role from her eyes.

Psalm 127:3 reveals that our children are more than a reflection of our own egos:

"Behold, children are a heritage from the Lord, the fruit of the womb a reward."

Matthew 18:4 tells us they can be an example for us:

"Whoever humbles himself like this child is the greatest in the kingdom of heaven."

Proverbs 22:6 tells us that (yes, this bears repeating) how our children turn out falls on our shoulders:

"Train up a child in the way he should go; even when he is old he will not depart from it."

Ethan Couch may lack the ability to understand the consequences of his actions, but his parents are right there with him. His father once impersonated a police officer and pulled his son out of school when officials questioned the boy driving himself to school at age 13. His mother left the country with her son to keep him from time behind bars.

Our kids come to us as blank slates, looking to us for guidance. However they turn out, they will have learned it from us.

When we follow the training we get from God, we will mature in the image of God.

Light Bulb Moment

Our submission unto God allows us to show love to the people who walk this life at our side.

Submitted to God

Strength and independence are the bywords of the day.

No one wants to be a wimp. We won't stand for anyone to kick sand in our face, and never, never, say a bad thing about our momma.

We won't stand for it, and rightly so. No one should have to endure such abuse.

Yet there are times we must give in. Taxes. We write the check no matter how much we don't like it. The speed limit applies to everyone. Diet? Must we? That slice of pie will enlarge our pant size if we don't pass it by.

What does God want us to submit to?

Ephesians 5:21 tells us not to run over our fellow believers even if we disagree with them.

"[Submit] to one another out of reverence for

Christ."

Ephesians 4:32 gives Christ as our example in treating others kindly.

> "Be kind to each other, tenderhearted, forgiving one another, as God in Christ forgave you."

Genesis 2:18, 21-22 says God sometimes needs to remove something from us before we're ready to fit perfectly with the spouse he has for us.

> "Then the LORD God said, 'It is not good that the man should be alone; I will make him a helper fit for him.' . . . So the LORD God caused a deep sleep to fall upon the man, and while he slept took one of his ribs and closed up its place with flesh. And the rib that the LORD God had taken from the man he made into a woman and brought her to the man."

1 Peter 3:7 is our commandment to treat our marriage (and our spouse) with the ultimate care and respect, if we want to show we're submitted fully unto God.

> "Likewise, husbands, live with your wives in an understanding way, showing honor to the woman as the weaker vessel, since they are heirs with you of the grace of life, so that your prayers may not be hindered."

Our strength and independence are outstanding character traits when used properly. When they interfere with our personal relationships, then we've valued them too highly. It's time to put them aside and become vulnerable for love.

Our submission unto God allows us to show love to the people who walk this life at our side.

Light Bulb Moment

Jesus is perfection; all else leads the wrong direction.

Surviving God's Fire

The name of Charles Goodyear is an icon in manufacturing. We see him scrawled across tires worldwide, clearly having found success due to his inventive mind and hard work.

Nothing could be further from the truth. Visions of wealth danced in Goodyear's head when he stumbled onto the secret to his manufacturing process in 1839, but the Goodyear Tire and Rubber Company was founded in his honor, and not by Charles Goodyear.

What had Goodyear done that we remember him for today? Until that time rubber was essentially useless, and the industry was in decline. The substance was brittle in winter and became a sticky goo in summer. It took many years and more borrowed money than he could ever repay before Goodyear accidentally hit on the process of vulcanization. Heat rubber enough, and it changes its properties. It becomes useful. This discovery turned the rubber industry around.

However, Goodyear received little compensation for the work he had done, and he died in 1860, $200,000 in debt.

Babylon was one of the most magnificent cities of the ancient age, housing the fabled Hanging Gardens, one of the Seven Wonders of the Ancient World.

Just as with Goodyear's process of vulcanization, it took a lot of work to build Babylon.

Yet, in Jeremiah 51:58 we read:

> "Thus says the Lord of hosts: The broad wall of Babylon shall be leveled to the ground, and her high gates shall be burned with fire. The peoples labor for nothing, and the nations weary themselves only for fire."

Today, the remnants of Babylon consist of broken mud-brick buildings about 50 miles south of Baghdad in modern-day Iraq. Only that which survived the fire remains.

What is the Babylon we spend our efforts building? Do we live in our Babylon? Drive our Babylon? Store up our Babylon in a wine cellar or in Swiss bank accounts?

The truth is that what we try to build is only for fire, for it will be destroyed in the end. Does that mean we should live in mud huts? That would be silly. Instead, we should remember what's important. It's not the house, the cars, the money. It's life, and we find true life in Jesus.

Charles Goodyear's rubber was only useful after it passed through the fire. Our lives are the same. After Goodyear lost everything, he wrote: "A man only has cause for regret when he sows and no one reaps." Goodyear knew the truth that fulfillment is not found in things but in the life we live in pursuit of those things.

Let's pursue Jesus, and we will gain that which cannot be destroyed by fire.

Jesus is perfection; all else leads the wrong direction.

Light Bulb Moment

Nine-tenths of Christianity is caring for those who walk at our side.

Taking Care of the Little Guy

Life on Four Strings is the compelling documentary of Jake Shimabukuro, a ukulele virtuoso who is an international icon in the world of music.

Yet, growing up, he had one job: take care of his younger brother.

Years later, Jake's mother apologized for working multiple jobs as a single mother and depriving her son of a real childhood. He laughed it off, saying it was his childhood, and he didn't feel deprived.

He took care of the little guy, and that was all right with him.

James 1:27 tells us:

> "Religion that is pure and undefiled before God, the Father, is this: to visit orphans and widows in their affliction, and to keep oneself unstained from the world."

God wants us to take care of the little guy. The picture is much bigger than just orphans and widows. We start there, sure, but we need to look so much further. How about the drug addict that has lost the ability to make good decisions? The church member that hasn't yet learned to control her tongue? Or the parent that interferes in our marriage?

These are all little guys, people that haven't matured in Christ. They may be older than we are, have more social prestige, or simply be undesirable, but in God's eyes, they need a helping hand so that they can grow in him to become more than they are.

Read in 1 Timothy 2:1-4:

> "First of all, then, I urge that supplications, prayers, intercessions, and thanksgivings be made for all people, for kings and all who are in high positions, that we may lead a peaceful and quiet life, godly and dignified in every way. This is good, and it is pleasing in the sight of God our Savior, who desires all people to be saved and to come to the knowledge of the truth."

There is no such thing as someone who is too far down any road to not need taking care of. From the most powerful world leaders to the homeless person on the street, we need to be like Jake Shimabukuro. If we take care of those around us, the world will be better, and we needn't feel deprived at all. We will be doing what Jesus would do if he walked at our side.

Nine-tenths of Christianity is caring for those who walk at our side.

Light Bulb Moment

Our undefiled marriage union bestows upon us God's ultimate honor.

The Highest Honor

We enjoy receiving honor.

In April of 2015, Sue, a long-time volunteer at the Azle Senior Center near Fort Worth, Texas, received special recognition for her services. She was justifiably proud. The center had recently undergone a change in leadership, and she had manned the helm full time—still in volunteer status—for months until a new director could be hired.

She wanted to tout her award around, to show it off to everyone she knew, so they could share in her glory.

Simpler things can be equally meaningful to us. Our insurance gives us a special discount for on-time payments. Our home receives the neighborhood Yard of the Month award. Our grandchildren gather to celebrate our 70th birthday. We are chosen by our peers as Teacher of the Year.

What's the big one? What's the top honor? Is it the

Nobel, to receive recognition from a world-class organization? To be elected President, the most powerful office in the world? Or maybe to win the lottery and receive a $100 million payout?

What makes our brain buzz with the excitement of the possibility?

The Word gives us a pretty good pointer to aim us the correct direction.

Genesis 2:24 tells us how to place ourselves in a position to receive recognition:

> "Therefore a man shall leave his father and his mother and hold fast to his wife, and they shall become one flesh."

For our insurance company to offer us the latest discounts, we have to first make our payments on time. Our home? There's hours of back-breaking toil before our yard is considered for an award. How many diapers have we changed before our grandchildren are grown enough to want to give back unto us?

The day of the wedding is just the first step. We still have a long way to go.

Hebrews 13:4 gives us our jubilation celebration opportunity:

> "Let marriage be held in honor among all, and

let the marriage bed be undefiled, for God will judge the sexually immoral and adulterous."

When we prove our marriage vows, we are lifted up before the world, and we deserve recognition. The couple holding hands at their 65th anniversary deserves higher honor than the most celebrated Nobel Prize winner. They hold a higher office than the President, and their faithfulness is worth more than the lottery's highest payout.

On our wedding day, our brains should buzz with the possibility.

Our undefiled marriage union bestows upon us God's ultimate honor.

Light Bulb Moment

When Christ is on the mound, we'll win every time.

Train Up a Child

The title today comes from Proverbs 22:6:

> "Train up a child in the way he should go; even when he is old he will not depart from it."

That's easily said, but how do we do it? How do we organize our child's life so that he will not depart from good teaching? What examples do we set? How do we live and love well enough that our message is instilled in her forever and ever? How can we hit a home run in raising our children to be good people?

Let's look at five scriptures from the Bible that cover all the bases.

First Base:

> Mark 12:30 must happen before anything else. Miss this one, and we're already out and off the field.

"And you shall love the Lord your God with all your heart and with all your soul and with all your mind and with all your strength."

Second Base:

Mark 12:31 puts us firmly on second. We have a Christian obligation to teach our children to treat others with kindness and compassion.

"The second is this: You shall love your neighbor as yourself. There is no other commandment greater than these."

Third Base:

John 8:32 reminds us that without knowing the rules of the game, we have no hope of reaching home plate. We must teach our children from the Word of God.

"And you will know the truth, and the truth will set you free."

Home Plate:

Deuteronomy 6:18 narrows our vision and ups the intensity of our game. We want our children to live the lessons they've been taught. They will follow the example we've set for them, good or bad.

"And you shall do what is right and good in the

sight of the Lord, that it may go well with you, and that you may go in and take possession of the good land that the Lord swore to give to your fathers."

The game isn't over just because we reach home plate. There is another level of the game, a pennant to win:

Proverbs 4:5 tells us how our children and grandchildren can be winners, also.

"Get wisdom; get insight; do not forget, and do not turn away from the words of my mouth."

Wisdom in the game of baseball comes from our coaches, from practice before the game, and from experience. In life, as parents, we are the coaches, we practice as a family, and we live out our lessons at play and in school.

It's the same in our Christian life. Christ is our coach, church is our practice session, and experience is what we get every day. Our children will win, bases loaded, a triple header, when their children also live for the Lord.

When Christ is on the mound, we'll win every time.

Light Bulb Moment

Our families are the pods, and we are the peas inside. How we treat the peas at our side impacts us also.

Two Peas Make a Pod

God desires us to have a more effective prayer life. To do that, we have to respect the peas that share our pod.

It's generally accepted that Peter wrote the books that bear his name. What was he trying to get across in 1 Peter 3:7?

> "Likewise, husbands, live with your wives in an understanding way, showing honor to the woman as the weaker vessel, since they are heirs with you of the grace of life, so that your prayers may not be hindered."

Peter knew there was discord and maybe disrespect among the husbands and wives in the body of believers. He wanted to offer his knowledge and understanding under the leading of the Spirit of God to give encouragement to his fellow believers. His words continue to offer encouragement that we must follow the teachings of Jesus rather than tradition or the ideas of men.

Two other disciples echo his sentiments.

John 13:34 tells us:

> "A new commandment I give to you, that you love one another: just as I have loved you, you also are to love one another."

Here John is telling us that love cherishes and is kind as well as protects the one loved.

We see this concept reflected in Matthew 19:19 as well:

> "Honor your father and mother, and, You shall love your neighbor as yourself."

In the comfort of a family living in close relationship, it's easy to forget to be kind when things are not going well. When trials come, it's easier to strike out at those we love, and feel they are at fault. Instead we should look in the mirror and examine ourselves to see if we are following the principles of love that Jesus taught.

1 Peter 3:1 continues to exhort us:

> "Likewise, wives, be subject to your own husbands, so that even if some do not obey the word, they may be won without a word by the conduct of their wives."

This tells the wives of his day that they were not putting love in their actions toward their husbands. When we love someone, we are willing to put them first over ourselves.

This brings us back to Verse 7, where Peter tells husbands to be considerate of their wives, as they are joint heirs of the gift of life. If we are joint heirs, we have equal rights. As we consider our own ideas and wants important, we also need to show that same consideration to our wives. We must treat them with the same respect we desire, and we must do so in love.

If we fail in this command, God is not pleased.

It's when we show our love that our prayers are not hindered, and we become more effective workers in the kingdom of God.

Our families are the pods, and we are the peas inside. How we treat the peas at our side impacts us also.

Light Bulb Moment

Showing love toward others isn't work when we view the world as our Lord does.

Weaving Love Into Our Lives

Weaving is amazing. We can take castoff fibers, no more than ragged remnants from other projects, and bring about useful items of beauty that will become cherished treasures.

It isn't easy, and it takes a long time. The weaver's hands must be skillful, inserting this thread here, and that thread there, to bring about the interplay of blues, reds, and yellows that paint the most incredible scenes. Back away a few steps, and the best of weavings will seem like a painting of indiscernible detail. The mixture of colors in the individual threads will blend so well that each one will melt into the next. We won't be able to tell where one stops and the next starts.

In effect, each thread becomes intrinsic to the next. We can't imagine the weaving without each one.

That is exactly how God weaves love into our lives.

Colossians 2:2 encourages us to bond one to another:

> "That their hearts may be encouraged, being knit together in love, to reach all the riches of full assurance of understanding and the knowledge of God's mystery, which is Christ."

1 Samuel 18:1 speaks to us of friendship:

> "As soon as he had finished speaking to Saul, the soul of Jonathan was knit to the soul of David, and Jonathan loved him as his own soul."

Genesis 34:3 draws us to the opposite sex:

> "And his soul was drawn to Dinah the daughter of Jacob. He loved the young woman and spoke tenderly to her."

Genesis 29:32 calls spouses to love one another:

> "And Leah conceived and bore a son, and she called his name Reuben, for she said, 'Because the Lord has looked upon my affliction; for now my husband will love me.' "

Genesis 25:28 is about love for our children:

> "Isaac loved Esau because he ate of his game, but Rebekah loved Jacob."

Genesis 24:67 tells of the comforting power of love:

> "Then Isaac brought her into the tent of Sarah

his mother and took Rebekah, and she became his wife, and he loved her. So Isaac was comforted after his mother's death."

1 John 4:8 says love is essential in our lives:

"Anyone who does not love does not know God, because God is love."

Hebrews 13:1 lets us know there is no end to love:

"Let brotherly love continue."

1 Thessalonians 5:26 is our greeting of love:

"Greet all the brothers with a holy kiss."

John 13:34 commands us to love one another:

"A new commandment I give to you, that you love one another: just as I have loved you, you also are to love one another."

1 Peter 3:8 rates love with the best of qualities we are to show:

"Finally, all of you, have unity of mind, sympathy, brotherly love, a tender heart, and a humble mind."

Jesus was our finest example of true love. He lived his life for those who could give him nothing in return, and then relinquished his life on the cross for people who weren't even born. Jesus loved because he could, not because he expected something in return. His love blended so well into his everyday life that his story has become the tapestry upon which we can base fruitful relationships every day of the year.

Showing love toward others isn't work when we view the world as our Lord does.

Light Bulb Moment

However we celebrate our love, if it's from the heart, there's no distance too far for us to go.

When We Fall in Love

That's about it, too. We fall into love, head over heels, like tripping into a chasm that swallows us wholly and completely.

The thing is, we don't want to climb out, either. We're happy in our love chasm. Even when we get bunged up along the way, it seems all right with us.

We're in love.

Solomon was the poet of love, a treasure to the romantic of heart, and our inspiration for azure evenings of fancy.

And the bride confesses her love . . .

> "Let him kiss me with the kisses of his mouth! For your love is better than wine." (Song of Solomon 1:2)

Her husband gives his adoring response . . .

> "Behold, you are beautiful, my love; behold, you

are beautiful; your eyes are doves. (Song of Solomon 1:15)

He continues with the words of an Egyptian endearment, calling to her as his sister-bride . . .

"You have captivated my heart, my sister, my bride; you have captivated my heart with one glance of your eyes, with one jewel of your necklace." (Song of Solomon 4:9)

The two lovers have fallen completely for one another, and nothing can separate them from each other's tender embrace.

Proverbs reveals the strength of our love attraction.

"Whoever covers an offense seeks love, but he who repeats a matter separates close friends." (Proverbs 17:9)

When we're in love, our adored one can spill soup in our lap, and we won't care. When we're not, nothing will cover the slightest offense.

Genesis and Ephesians tell how deeply our love will flow when we find our true helpmeet.

"So Jacob served seven years for Rachel, and they seemed to him but a few days because of the love he had for her." (Genesis 29:20)

"Husbands, love your wives, as Christ loved the

church and gave himself up for her." (Ephesians 5:25)

No price is too great to offer for the one we love, whether seven years or our very life.

We express our love in hearts and flowers, XXXs and OOOs. We blow kisses, hold hands, and gaze with adoring moon eyes at our love. Then there's chocolate, diamonds, and a night on the town.

However we celebrate our love, if it's from the heart, there's no distance too far for us to go.

Coming to Christ
In Three Easy Steps

If you do not know Christ as your personal savior, there is no better time than the present to turn your life over to him.

- ➤ Step 1 is to admit that you are human, God is God, and you need his grace.
- ➤ Step 2 is to place your belief in him. You must accept that he is the Son of the Eternal God, and through his death on the cross, he can give you new life.
- ➤ Step 3 is to turn from your previous ways and receive the hope of Jesus' power in you.

Fill in the following information as a testament to your decision to accept Jesus as your Savior.

I, _____, accept Jesus
            print your full name

as my personal savior on _____.
                             today's date

_____
                    your signature

Look for these additional topics on the MyChurchNotes.net website:

2 Timothy
Beatitudes
Discipleship
Evangelism
Faith
Family
Healing
Hope
Kingdom of God
Money
Prayer
Relationships
Repentance
Salvation
Worship

MyChurchNotes.net is a faith-based ministry founded on a belief in the Father, the Son, and the Holy Spirit. All MyChurchNotes.net articles are based on Scripture and created especially for MyChurchNotes.net.

Our Mission Statement is to take the Word of God into all the nations, and proclaim that he is Lord!

If you enjoyed
God Wraps Our Family in Love,
please visit us at our website:

www.MyChurchNotes.net

We look forward to hearing from you.

Website and Publication Powered by:

Bright Herd . . . for All Your Website and Media Design Needs.
www.brightherd.com
contact@brightherd.com

www.ingramcontent.com/pod-product-compliance
Lightning Source LLC
LaVergne TN
LVHW051835080426
835512LV00018B/2895